Manchester

Dear Reader

 Thank you for picking up the book. There are a few things that I'd like to say before you go any further.

 It doesn't matter what order you read it in — just dip in wherever it appeals to you!

 If I have any qualification at all for writing this book, it is simply that, for the last 6-7 years, I have been deeply involved with young people who are struggling to work out what commitment to Jesus means in their everyday lives.

 I want to say thank you to the Platters for their help. They are a fine crowd of ordinary young people — many of them appear in the pages that follow.

 I hope the book will be a help to some people at least. If you reckon I'm wrong in places (I may well be!) or if I haven't helped you with your problems, do dig out someone who can help — or even write to me, c/o Scripture Union.

   Christopher Irish

P.S. Thank you Joan, Brigid & Anne for doing so much typing — so willingly — and Pam (my wife) for your honest advice and encouragement. You were usually right!

4

I BELONG

I belong to him.

I know it doesn't seem to make sense, but the person I belong to lived the best part of two thousand years ago. When he died, aged only 33, he was more or less unknown outside his own country in the Middle East.

He had caused no small stir, however. Born in the most humble of places, brought up to be a carpenter, he led a quiet, unspectacular life until he was 30. Then followed three explosive years.

He began to *teach*. He taught from everyday things,

Being a Christian today

by Christopher Frith

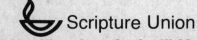

Scripture Union

47 Marylebone Lane, London W1M 6AX

Printed by Coloprint, Hutton, Weston-super-Mare

"I BELONG"

FOREWORD

I am glad to write this short introduction to Christopher Frith's book because it is always exciting to read what is written by a young clergyman deeply involved with young people and sympathetic to the wide variety of their needs and aspirations. This book is written from within his own energetic experience of leading young people to faith in Christ; answering their questions on a variety of subjects; and seeking bravely to help them through the complexities of today's world.

I imagine that some older people may raise their eyebrows because Christopher Frith tackles explicitly the real problems that press upon boys and girls today and he writes from the heart of successful parochial ministry. He is brave enough to try to give Christian answers to questions people are *really* asking. I am glad to commend this book, and I hope it will help many young people to faith in Christ and practical Christian witness and service.

Maurice Norvic
The Bishop's House
Norwich

First published 1977 by Scripture Union, 47 Marylebone Lane, London W1M 6AX

ISBN 0 85421 506 9

Unless otherwise specified, Bible references are taken from the Good News Bible, ©American Bible Society, British and Foreign Bible Society and William Collins Sons & Co. Ltd.

Designed by Carey Procter

everyday happenings, everyday people. And people by the
thousands showed their hunger to learn. They learnt that life
was worth more than things like food and clothing. They
learnt that love meant being kind to those who were horrible
to them. And they learnt that there was a real Father in
heaven who could be trusted to look after them.

He began to *heal*. No human need, however squalid,
escaped him, and, wherever people would trust him, he gave
them wholeness. Thousands found a new life — the blind and
the lame, the leper and the demon-possessed, the swindling

tax collector and the flagrant adultress. . . . Body, mind and spirit were all healed by him.

He began to be *tracked down*. A dangerous man to have around, he even claimed to forgive people's sin. This was as good as saying that he was God, which, according to the religious experts, was utterly impossible. So, he had to be trapped and done away with.

He was *executed*. After an illegal trial, with no concrete evidence, he was condemned to die the death of a common criminal. The charge? Blasphemy — a religious offence for which Roman law did not allow the death penalty.

He *came back to life*. To the acute embarrassment of all his opponents from that day on he was seen by numerous eye-witnesses. His body bore the scars of his execution; it was undoubtedly him. He proceeded to spend time with his followers, who had once been desperate with fear but were now beside themselves with joy. He assured them that they belonged to him for ever and sent them all over the world inviting everyone to belong to him.

His final words were these: 'And remember! I will be with you always'.

His name? JESUS — meaning, the rescuer of mankind.

"All-or-nothing people"

I belong to him, to Jesus. I, too, have met him. I haven't seen him but I know he's alive today. Because I belong to him, and know he accepts me, I am passionately committed to him and to what he wants me to do.

Every true Christian belongs to Jesus in this personal, individual way. And when we do belong to Jesus, we belong to each other, as well.

Jesus said that becoming a Christian meant calling God 'Father'. In fact, he called him 'Abba' — a word which really means 'Dad'. If we're in his family, God is our 'Dad'. Our past is forgiven and forgotten, God knows us as his children in his family, and we see each other as brothers and sisters. So, not only do I belong to Jesus, I also belong to my fellow brothers and sisters. And together, bit by bit, we find ourselves taking on the family likeness and becoming more like Jesus.

We can't get away from it. It's a tremendous privilege to belong to this family. But you never get *privileges* without *responsibilities*. We could sum up these responsibilities this way — we must be '*all-or-nothing people*'. Jesus says some hard words to 'half-and-half' people. 'I know that you are neither cold nor hot. How I wish that you were either one or the other! But, because you are barely warm, neither hot nor cold, I am going to spit you out of my mouth!' (Revelation 3.15,16)

These words don't fit the 'meek and the mild' image of Jesus, somehow. Read this: 'You blind fools . . . snakes and sons of snakes . . . you are like whitewashed tombs . . . fine on the outside but full of dead men's bones . . . you are children of your father, the devil . . .' (See Matthew chapter 23)

Who did Jesus get so angry with? Always, it was with hypocrites, and religious hypocrites at that — those who pretended to be what they weren't. It's the same today. If we're

Christians and belong to Jesus (our privilege), we must show it (our responsibility). It's no good pretending to belong to him if we don't live for him.

So these are the privileges:

I belong to Jesus.

I belong to the family of God.

I belong to my Christian brothers and sisters.

And the responsibilities? The rest of this book is about them.

You will probably know the *Spinners* song, *The Family of Man*. Try changing the words and singing about *The Family of God*. (With apologies to Fred Dallas, who wrote the original song.)

We belong to a family, the greatest on earth;
More and more each day are coming to birth;
We're a family of love and peace and joy,
We're a family that Satan can't destroy.
> We're the family of God — keep growing —
> The family of God — keep sowing
> The seeds of new life every day.

We're modelled on our Master, following his call,
The greatest on earth but the least of all,
Denying ourselves, the slaves of each other,
And love, love, love, love our brother.
> We're the family of God . . .

We're all one body, Jesus our head,
Living our lives by the words he's said:
'Be wise as a serpent, harmless as a dove,
Covering the world with a blanket of love'.
> We're the family of God . . . .

1 Why do you think that Jesus was not forgotten soon after he died, like most people are?

2 In what ways have you discovered that Jesus' words, 'I will be with you always . . .' are true?

3 How would you describe the 'family likeness' of the family of God?

Things to talk or think about

GET STUCK IN

Kevin is a gardener, used to his own company and rather enjoying it. One evening, he was walking through a park when he discovered a man called Arthur Blessitt, the American evangelist, preaching to a big crowd. It was just curiosity at first which made him join them all — but by the end of that evening, Kevin had given his life to Jesus Christ.

'Mind you,' he says, 'I didn't know what I'd done, really, at first. I had to go away and think about it all. Perhaps I did too much thinking, at work and that. . . . But soon I realized I'd got to get stuck in, really get involved. It was no good waiting for things to happen.'

What did he mean by getting stuck in?

He went on:

'First of all, it was reading the Bible, even when I was at work . . . but I'm thinking more of getting stuck in with the youth work at the church and the people at the church, not just being a spectator or visitor.' (Incidentally, Kevin had had no previous connection with the church.)

'It's like anything else, isn't it really? It's like your job or making friends — you have to apply yourself. You know, you have to work at it — it's the same way with Christianity. I've found it's up to what you put in, what you get out. But it's easy to be half-hearted.'

'The trouble is that life is so big and the way we look at Christianity is so small. It doesn't cover everything . . . so many areas of life where God should be and where he isn't. Unless it's every bit of your life that's involved with your Christianity, with Christ, you easily go off the rails.'

Kevin set me thinking about how important it is to be utterly and completely committed to Jesus. No half measures. Jesus himself made this point time and time again. It was like being a farmer: 'Anyone who starts to plough and then keeps looking back is of no use for the Kingdom of God.' (Luke 9.62)

Love is His Lifestyle

Total involvement with Jesus means a totally different life-style.

Love is his life-style. This means being DIFFERENT:

Different

because really loving people isn't usual;

Different

because really loving God means not doing some things which many think are 'normal';

Different

because we're to be deeply involved with people and their many needs;

Different

because we're to be deeply involved with fellow-Christians because God has made them our brothers and sisters;

Different

because we're to be deeply involved with God and aim to get to know him better and better:

Different

because the aim of our lives is to worship and please God.

What has Jesus Christ in common with the world of 'pop'?

Since *Godspell* and *Jesus Christ Superstar* came on the scene, this hasn't seemed quite such a stupid question as it was before. The answer, now, is quite easy; the favourite word of both is LOVE. Love is the message of the average pop song and it certainly sums up the message of Jesus.

But there's all the difference in the world when it comes to what they both mean by love. 'Pop-love' or '20th century love' even, as we might call it, has many fine things about it. But, in the end, it usually means loving those who seem to deserve it — 'I love everyone I choose to love', or even 'I love everyone . . . except my parents'. With Jesus, there can be no *except*. His love has nothing whatsoever to do with the attractiveness of the one who receives it, nor with deserving it. And it involves self-giving, self-sacrifice.

LONG LIVE LOVE!

'Long live love . . . love is to care, caring and sharing, long live love', went the jingle-jangle of the United Kingdom's 1974 entry for the Eurovision Song Contest. Not even a face as pretty as Olivia Newton-John's could persuade the judges to make the song a winner, but the chorus does, in fact, approach the sort of love Jesus taught about. If we really care, if we really share (that is, do something about it) then we really love.

The trouble is, it sounds nice and pleasant — even easy. But what did Jesus, in fact, say?

1. Love Your Enemy

'Love your enemies, do good to those who hate you, bless those who curse you and pray for those who mistreat you.' (Luke 6.27,28)

Films about the second world war are still very popular. A television serial like *Colditz* gathered a large audience. But is it right to be still harking back to war-time? Doesn't it arouse hostility towards our old opponents? It can hardly help British people to love German people, and vice-versa.

Even if it is not another nation, who are your real enemies? It could be your boss. It could be your older sister or perhaps the person who let your best-kept secret out so that you're teased about it now. It could be the one who has the place you deserve in the football team, or the girl who is going out with the boy you fancy. Or it could be the person who murdered your father, who beat you up so badly that you will never recover fully, or who drove his car headlong into yours when he was stone-drunk.

Jesus asks the impossible. Love that person. Do him a good turn. Pray for him. And you can't do any of this without *forgiving* him. Jesus himself did it. He showed us what loving your enemies means.

2. Love Your Neighbour

'You must love your neighbour as yourself.' (Mark 12.31)

My neighbour is my fellow human being. Often it can be just as hard, just as demanding, to love *him* as to love my enemy. Jesus leaves no room for the things which are typical of human nature. For instance:–

Prejudice What does the colour of a person's skin matter? If Christians don't set a lead in declaring that all colour prejudice is evil, in encouraging trust in each other and in breaking down barriers, who will? Suspicion will grow. So will violence.

People must be treated as people — not as black or white, Catholic or Protestant, even North and South. In Manchester, people from 'down south' tend to be written off as 'toffee-nosed'. Northerners, in turn, are written off as 'Philistines' and neither takes the other seriously.

Snobbery Just because someone is different, we tend to reject him or her. But think how different Jesus' disciples were from each other. Fishermen (like Peter) mixed happily with an ardent politician (Simon the Zealot) and a tax-collector (Matthew). For the Christian, social barriers are there to be ignored. It is just as wrong to say 'I wouldn't dream of speaking to her — she goes to a posh boarding school', as to say, 'I can't stand people who eat fish and chips with their fingers out of newspaper'. It is wrong to look down our noses no matter who is beneath them. It may be a drug addict or it may be someone who dresses terribly. Jesus says, 'Accept that person, do all you can to help him or her; love him.'

The Generation Gap This seems to be a feature of life today — especially within families. Many teenagers (Christians included) seem to reject home. It is unfashionable to enjoy a good relationship with parents and grandparents — and often with brothers and sisters, too. But, if you can't put your Christianity into practice where you live, where people can see what you are really like, the seriousness of your faith must be doubted. Many parents are a bit unreasonable; they find it hard to understand their children. But Jesus added his full authority to the Ten Commandments — including the fifth: 'Honour your father and mother'. (Exodus 20.12)

In a healthy community, the elderly respect the young for their enthusiasm and new ideas, and the young respect the wisdom and experience of those who have been around long enough to pick it all up.

Ignoring those in need Everywhere, there are elderly people, often very lonely, unable to get out, with only a television to talk to. Regular visits from a young person can

"Encourage trust"

make an old person's life worth living. Or what about handicapped people? Or invalids? Or the blind? Or the starving in many parts of the world?

Not everyone can actually go overseas to help. But, all young people can raise money for causes such as Christian Aid and TEAR Fund. Do you love enough for it to cost something: some time, some effort, some money?

Need isn't only physical. Everyone has a spiritual need — a need of Jesus Christ. As well as trying to love in a practical way, our great aim must be to help people to become Christians. It is, of course, utterly wrong to help people in need only because we want to convert them, but it is just as wrong *not* to be interested in their spiritual position. Jesus loves us completely, *the whole of us,* our bodies and our spirits. His is the example to follow.

3 Love your brother and sister in Christ

'A new commandment I give to you: love one another. As I have loved you, so you must love one another.' (John 13.34)

If you go on a Christian camp or holiday venture and meet up with complete strangers who are also Christians, you will be struck by one of the most marvellous of all the experiences which Jesus gives us. We have the same Heavenly Father, the same Saviour, and the same Holy Spirit within us, and so we have everything in common. We may never have met before. We may be totally different sorts of people. Different races. Even speaking different languages. But we can be united. We can know something deeper than friendship. It is the love of Jesus.

This sort of love, for our brothers and sisters in Christ, is emphasized above all others in the New Testament. But, look out! It easily grows cold and becomes scarcely noticeable. Christians fall out with each other and the Church gets noted more for its squabbling than its unity. And when there is no unity, God's work is held up. When there *is* unity, when there is fellowship, when the love of Jesus can be seen amongst those who really know him — then people are interested. They want to know what it's all about. They can see something worth having.

4 Love the Lord your God

'You must love the Lord your God with all your heart, and with all your soul, and with all your mind, and with all your strength.' (Mark 12.30)

Like all Jesus' teaching about love, this is tremendously demanding. It sounds nice and cosy to say 'I love God' — but stop to think. It involves every part of your life — your heart (what you feel), your soul (what you pray), your mind (what you think) and your strength (what you do). Several times, Jesus taught that loving God means *obeying* him. Obedience isn't a fashionable word, like love, but they have to go hand in hand. (See John 14.21)

Do you feel overwhelmed by all this? Do you, as I do, find a fifth kind of love coming much more easily — LOVE YOURSELF?

Here is some encouragement:—

Remember: Love often starts in a small way, like being kind to *one* other person or obeying God in *one* small matter when previously you have disobeyed him.

Remember: If we're Christians, we have Jesus with us. And Jesus is all about love; in fact the Bible says he *is* love. He'll show us how to love and, most important, he'll help us to love.

"Loving God means obeying God"

1 How would you describe the difference between 'pop-love' and Jesus' love, as mentioned previously? What are the good things about 'pop-love'?

2 Who are *your* enemies? How do you set about loving them?

3 Do you think that loving people means always giving them what they want?

4 Read 1 Corinthians 13.4-7. Try putting your own name instead of the word 'love'. Could you describe yourself as a loving person by these standards?

Things to talk or think about

WIND AND FIRE

A test of whether or not you are a Christian is to ask yourself: 'Do I possess the Holy Spirit?' 'Whoever does not have the Spirit of Christ does not belong to him,' said St. Paul. (Romans 8.9)

Becoming a Christian involves receiving the Spirit of Jesus, the Holy Spirit, into your life. If there is any change in your life (and there should be) that is the work of the Holy Spirit.

Well, who is the Holy Spirit? This is a very natural question to ask. Even when we are at our most intelligent best, it is difficult to understand who *God* is.

God the Father is all right when we think of the all-powerful God who made the universe — even if it does seem impossible for him to be interested in everyone, all over the world, at the same time.

But we *can* picture *God the Son* (the Lord Jesus) because he came to earth as a human being, even if we are bamboozled by him being God and man at the same time.

But *God the Holy Spirit* — who is he?

Let's go back to the day when the Holy Spirit first came to the disciples — the Day of Pentecost.

They were all together in Jerusalem. They knew that Jesus had risen from the dead. They knew that they had a mission, as Jesus had told them to 'go to all peoples everywhere and make them my disciples'. (Matthew 28.19) But, as yet, it was a mission impossible. They couldn't do it. They were just ordinary people. They hadn't the power.

They knew that one day they *would* have the power. Jesus' last words to them had been these: 'You will be filled with power when the Holy Spirit comes on you, and you will be witnesses for me. . . .' (Acts 1.8) They were waiting.

THE HOLY SPIRIT

Then the drama began. A mighty wind swept through the place. Tongues of fire appeared on them all. The Holy Spirit had come. They were different people. The timid became bold. The uneducated became brilliant preachers. All the barriers stopping the spread of the Good News were lifted. *That day the Church was founded.* About 3,000 people were converted. *Now* they had power!

That's who God the Holy Spirit is: the unseen power of God, the one who revolutionizes our lives, who stirs us into action, who comes to live inside us. But remember, although we can't see or picture him, he is still God, he is a person, and we mustn't call him 'it'.

He appeared in this spectacular way to enable us to understand him a bit, to realize the sort of thing he came to do.

Wind

The wind is a funny thing. You can never see it, but you know all right when it's blowing. You can feel it. You can see the effects of it. You can't stop it. You can't predict much about it. You don't know when it will change direction.

Now can you see why the Holy Spirit came as a strong wind? You don't see him, but you know all right when he is there. You can feel his presence. You can see the effects of his work. You can't stop him. You can't predict what he'll do. You don't know when he'll change direction and act in new and different ways.

Christian life is 'life in the Spirit', and that's why it's exciting. We could sum up the wind-like effect of the Holy Spirit in one word: *power*.

When Jesus talked about the power of the Holy Spirit, he

used a word which makes people think of explosions. The power available to every Christian is explosive.

Power to be witnesses for Jesus

The Holy Spirit is there to overcome our shyness. He's there to make us sure that what we're saying is true. He's there to help us when we're stumped for words. He's there to make us sensitive to people's real needs. And he's there to make people understand their need of the Good News.

Jesus spent a lot of time talking to his disciples about the Spirit, before his crucifixion. He called him the helper, or counsellor. 'When he comes he will prove to the people of the world that they are wrong about sin, and about what is right and about God's judgement' (John 16.8), Jesus told them. We should pray for the Holy Spirit to be doing his work as we speak for Jesus. Otherwise, everything we do and say for him will be useless.

Power in our everyday lives

How can I be more like Jesus? This has to be the work of his Spirit in your life.

How can I resist temptation? The Spirit of Jesus is always available, there inside you, to give you will-power.

"The Spirit makes God real"

How can I pray effectively? The Spirit of Jesus wants to help you to talk to God as well as to hear and understand God speaking to you.

How can I be sure I'm a Christian? The Spirit of Jesus has one job above all others: to make God real to us and to make us know Jesus is with us.

How does the Holy Spirit do these things?

He does them as we . . . ask him to.

. . . read the Bible.

. . . keep in with other Christians.

. . . get on with living, *expecting* the Holy Spirit to help.

Sometimes, we'll notice him (like an explosion).

Sometimes, we won't even know he's working (like the power which makes a baby grow). He works in different ways at different times and in different people.

To some, he gives particular gifts not given to everyone. For instance, some can do miraculous things, such as healing. Some have special wisdom. Some are given a special language to use in prayer to God (called 'speaking in tongues'). The important thing is that God the Holy Spirit gives these gifts to those he chooses. And they are to help us in our life together to bring glory to God.

We mustn't fall into the trap of wanting spectacular experiences for their own sake. Non-Christians are sometimes able to do these things; they are no proof, *on their own,* that someone is a Christian, let alone a special Christian. Jesus warned that many would try to get into heaven on the strength of such things: 'Many will say to me, "Lord, Lord! In your name, we spoke God's message, by your name we drove out many demons and performed many miracles!" Then I will say to them, "I never knew you. Get away from me, you wicked people!"' (Matthew 7.22,23)

Fire

Fire can be even more terrifying than wind. When the Holy Spirit came as tongues of fire, two things happened:

1 It showed the presence of God. He is utterly pure and holy. He cannot stand anything impure and unholy.

2 It showed that when God the Holy Spirit comes to live in our lives, he comes to burn away all that is rotten and evil. He comes to make us more like Jesus.

That is why you can tell a genuine Christian by the life he or she lives. It is a life made holy (separate, different, pure) by the Holy Spirit.

So, as the Holy Spirit burns away rottenness from our lives, he replaces it with the exact opposite, with beautiful things. Someone who is filled with God's Spirit is really distinctive — a beautiful person. That's why Jesus stood out from the crowd.

As well as Wind and Fire, think of another picture: fruit.

Fruit

St. Paul has a beautiful idea of the Christian life being like a fruit tree producing good fruit. This is what he says: 'The fruit of the Spirit is love, joy, peace, patience, kindness, goodness, faithfulness, gentleness, self-control'. (Galatians 5.22-23 RSV) Your life is the tree and your actions, words and thoughts are the fruit. As the fruit grows, it takes on different appearances; sometimes it's joy, sometimes love and so on, but it all comes from the Holy Spirit. Just as a tree doesn't make its own fruit grow, but the sap or life within it does, so we don't make the fruit of the Spirit grow: it's the work of the life within us, the Holy Spirit. Our job is just to do and be what he wants, in his strength.

Look at this list of the fruit of the Spirit again. It describes the life of Jesus perfectly.

Make a note of those nine things which make up the fruit of the Spirit. (Galatians 5.22-23) Try to learn them off by heart, and ask God the Holy Spirit to make them all appear more in your life.

Something to do

Look up these verses in your Bible and decide what they teach about the work of the Holy Spirit: John 3.1-8, John 15.26, John 16.13, John 16.14.

Something to talk or think about

HAVE I GOT TO GO TO CHURCH?

I CAN BE A PERFECTLY GOOD CHRISTIAN WITHOUT GOING TO CHURCH, THANKS VERY MUCH!

YOUR BLOOMIN' CHURCHES ARE FULL OF HYPOCRITES — HOLY ON SUNDAYS AND WORSE THAN THE REST OF US DURING THE WEEK.

THE CHURCH IS OUT OF TOUCH — STILL LIVING IN THE 17TH CENTURY!

We went carol singing round some pubs in Manchester one Christmas. These were some of the comments we got. There's a little truth in them, sadly, but the trouble is . . .
. . . most people haven't been to a church service in their lives;
. . . they don't know what the church *is*;
. . . they don't know what the church is *for*.

As you probably realize, the church hasn't got a very good image. But that's no reason for ignoring it.

What is the church?

The church is *people*.
It's not a building. It's not an institution.
It's the *Family of God*.
When Jesus taught his disciples to pray, he told them to say, 'Our Father . . .', not '*my* Father'. He was expecting there

to be different people, lots of very different people, all together, united by having *one* Father.

As in any human family, there are the peculiar members and the normal ones, the young ones and the old ones, the classical ones and the pop ones, the healthy ones and the weak ones. . . . All sorts of possible barriers. Every reason for misunderstanding.

But, we all say, 'Our Father in Heaven . . .' It's the Father who makes the Christian family into a family. He really understands each member. He loves us all equally. And we all have the same standing in his eyes. We all belong to the family — like it or not.

So, it makes sense that we should meet (and have a building in which to meet). Despite the generation gap and all the other gaps, we're all brothers and sisters; we belong to each other and we can accept and understand each other. If you avoid your own brothers and sisters, there's something wrong.

The Christian family, naturally, finds that it wants to meet together. And, as we do meet, we experience one of the most wonderful of all God's gifts: *fellowship.*

This means friendship with a difference, friendship with a depth not found anywhere else — the Christian family feeling.

However, despite this ideal of oneness, the sad thing is that the church today is divided into different denominations which don't agree with each other. But these divisions are gradually breaking down now, and each member can play his or her part in furthering this coming together. It's no excuse for opting out. You belong already, if you are a Christian.

We have said that it is natural for members of the Christian family to want to meet together. But what's the point of it? What do we do together that we can't do on our own? This question boils down to . . .

What is the church for?

It really has three purposes. They are all vital and they answer our friends in the pub: you *can't* be a perfectly good Christian on your own; you *can't* avoid joining in with other Christians; you *need* the rest of the family.

Purpose 1 To help and encourage each other

Being a Christian is difficult. It demands a lot of you. And, if you try and do it on your own, it's twice as difficult.

Jesus called his first followers as a group — and kept them together. This way, they were able to encourage each other.

Perhaps you don't think you need this. But suppose your best friend goes into hospital? Or you start having real difficulty praying? Or things are happening at work or school which worry you and you need to talk about them with someone? Or you fall in love and wonder if it's right?

At times like these, you need *support.* And God's way of

"Friendship with a difference"

giving support is through other members of the family. This can be either the Christian family at school or work (such as a Christian Union) or at home (the local church). It doesn't work, of course, unless we are *honest* about ourselves, unless we genuinely *share* our needs. But it's when we do this (and when we *listen* to what other members need to tell *us*) that we really experience fellowship — the Christian family feeling.

Purpose 2 To help others

We can do this on our own, but not nearly as effectively as when we unite together.

It has been said that the church is the only society or club which exists mainly for the benefit of non-members.

Obviously, members gain a lot from belonging to the church, in practical caring, understanding and friendship, as well as worship and teaching. But it is non-members who should be our main concern. The church's responsibility is to *show the love of God.*

This means being on the spot wherever there is need. Being generous to those who lack food, love, company, justice, etc. Being concerned to share the Good News of Jesus with anyone who will listen. Showing that Jesus is alive today.

"Show God's love"

True, the church has failed in this, time and again. Often we seem to show the exact opposite. But, here's the challenge for *you* and *your* church!

Purpose 3. To worship God

It is here, above all, that the family feeling comes in. The key person in any family is dad, and none more so than the Father of the Christian family. Because we, his children, love him, we need to express our love, and this is the Christian's main aim in life.

Of course, there are many, many different ways of telling God that we love him — that's really what worshipping him is. We can (and should) worship on our own. In a sense, our whole life must be worship of God. But the Bible always thinks of worship as something *done with others.* 'O magnify the Lord with me, let us praise his name *together,'* said the Psalmist.

This will involve **singing.** There's no better way, surely, to praise God than in song. If you can't sing in tune, don't worry. We're called to make a 'joyful noise' to God — it doesn't say 'tuneful'. But, if you can't stand singing, you can still praise God in words for all he is and all he has done.

It will involve **praying.** Jesus said that when people pray in his name, 'I am there with them'. Learning to pray with other Christians is a great experience — perhaps in a small group in a house, perhaps in a larger church prayer meeting. Don't be frightened of praying out loud — you're praying to God, not to the others there. Ask the Holy Spirit to lead you.

It will involve **Holy Communion,** or the Lord's Supper.

Shortly before he died, the Lord Jesus passed some bread and some wine round to all the disciples. He told them: 'Do this in memory of me'. Ever since, Christians have met together to share bread and wine. It is the most moving of all worship as we remember together the life, death and coming alive again of Jesus. Through it, we find God to be extra specially real. Because it is a *special* service, we need to come to it in the right frame of mind.

It will involve **learning** more about our Father and more about the Bible. And it is easiest and most enjoyable to do this with other members of the family. Often the small informal Bible Study group is best. It's a marvellous way to learn and to share problems, experiences and what God has been teaching us.

And it *is* possible — it really is — to learn from sermons in church services. Try asking God to help you to understand and listening carefully to what is said. If you *don't* understand, go and ask the minister what he meant after the service. If you have to do this every week, he'll soon get the message.

A Question

Q. I find I'm bored by church services and I don't feel welcome. Do I have to go?

A. I sympathize. Many churches are out-dated and hard to fit into. You were certainly right to give it a go. If you really can't fit in, try to find at least a few other Christians you do get on with and get them to help you to worship God and serve people. But, your aim should be, before too long, to belong to a local church. You may be able to change things a bit. And remember, it takes time to get used to the family you've been adopted into. Perhaps it takes them even longer to get used to you!

A Warning

Jesus quoted these words to hypocrites of his day: 'These people, says God, honour me with their words, but their heart is really far away from me.' (Mark 7.6)

Don't be a hypocrite of our day.

But, at the same time, don't use this as another excuse for not joining the family. There are many snares, many difficulties. But it is certainly worth facing them all. The other day, I asked a group of a dozen or so young people what was the most important thing which had helped them keep going in their Christian lives. All of them replied: *'fellowship'*.

You can't do without it.

1 Do you think it's wrong to want fellowship only with people of your own age?
2 Whose fault is the generation gap in church?
3 In the Family of God, what's your job? Could you do more?
4 Which of the three purposes of the church do you find is the most neglected?

Things to think and talk about

NAME YOUR

Question 1

Paul: 'Our youth group only seems to have religious activities. Shouldn't we be concerned about the needs of people around us?'

I agree, entirely. It is impossible to obey the command of Jesus to love our neighbour as ourselves if we shut our eyes to our neighbour's needs. What I suggest you do is:

1 Get some good ideas of what should be done.
2 Push the leader, the committee and all the members to get on and co-operate.
3 Set an example by taking the lead.

'What kind of things can we do?' you may well ask. Well, there's no limit, really. Let me suggest just a few ideas.

A *sponsored fast* could raise money (and publicity, too) for the millions who starve — who can have an easy conscience about possessing so many luxuries and earning so much money when people in other parts of the world have nothing?

A *painting and decorating team* could brighten up many an old person's house.

A *protest march* or numerous complaints to the Town Hall could draw attention to landlords (possibly the local Council) who fail to provide adequate housing conditions.

A *mass collection* of old newspapers in your area for recycling could raise money for some worthwhile project.

I'm sure you can add a lot more to the list.

Question 2

Pat: 'When I first became a committed Christian, Jesus seemed real to me. Now, a year or two later, I begin to wonder whether he is so real after all. Why do you think I have these doubts?'

In the end, it is because there's a devil and he doesn't like people trusting in Jesus Christ. Some people seem to be prone to doubt more than others and the devil has a whale of a time with those of us who do.

The first thing to say is that it can be a good, healthy thing to doubt. Nearly all Christians do doubt at one time or another and, after emerging from such a time, we often find that we have been strengthened in our faith.

However, we have no right to expect Jesus to be real to us if we make no attempt to keep close to him. It is possible to play into the devil's hands. If the only literature which you

HANG UP

ever read is atheist propaganda, you shouldn't be surprised when you begin to doubt Christianity! If you stop meeting with other Christians, if you rarely pray and read the Bible, or if you continue a life of sin, of course Jesus won't seem real to you.

John the Baptist doubted Jesus at one time. Mind you, he was in prison, and a Middle East prison in those days was a likely setting for depression and doubt. He would have been without fellowship and probably without the Scriptures. In despair he sent a message to Jesus: 'Are you really the Christ, or not?'

Jesus replied, 'Just look and see all that is going on around me. Just as was prophesied, the blind can see, the lame walk. . . .'

Look at Jesus; we can't get away from him and all the evidence that his claims are true. Look at those whose lives are being changed by him today. If you don't see this personally, you could read a biography of someone in whom God is working — your minister or youth leader would probably recommend such a book.

If you doubt, you can either face your doubts yourself — honestly and squarely with sympathetic Christians and with God himself — *or* you can use them as a good excuse for laziness and apathy.

Question 3

Derek: 'I became a Christian two years ago and I felt really guilty about smoking. People said: "You are a temple of the Holy Spirit. Why do you smoke?"
Surely, if God wanted me to give it up, I would be able to without any trouble because I know he could help me. But, until he calls me to stop, then I'll carry on smoking (twenty-five a day). If I gave it up myself I would just become miserable and temperamental.'

You're not alone, Derek. Hundreds have your problem! It can easily get out of proportion and seem like a terrible sin. I think that for most people smoking isn't a sin, but it could well be a hindrance.

I fear I am prejudiced; smoke always makes me cough. But stop and think; it is a strange habit, isn't it? The American comedian Bob Newhart has an item when he pretends to receive a phone call from Sir Walter Raleigh who is reporting

the discovery of tobacco. It sounds too ridiculous for words — you get leaves, shred them up, put the shreds on a piece of paper, roll it up, put it between your lips and then — wait for it — you set fire to it. Crazy!

Ask yourself these questions:

1 Can you really afford to burn away so much money? Think what else you could usefully do with the money.

2 Do you really want to risk lung cancer? Perhaps you haven't witnessed the suffering of someone who is dying of cancer.

You may, of course, be convinced about all this anyway. Your real question may be: 'How can I break the habit?' Do you really believe that God can give you the strength to do it? If so, ask for it and go ahead, believing he has given it to you. Get your Christian friends to help you, in prayer and encouragement. But, above all, trust the Lord. Leave the problem to him.

Question 4

Syd: 'When people go into church before a service, they always seem to pray quietly. It has always bothered me as I don't know what I'm supposed to pray about!'

I asked a few young Christians what they recommended:

Peter: 'It's just a convention. You don't have to do it if you don't want to.'

Christine: 'Sunday evening service is my big "come back to Jesus" time in the week, so I just like to get right with him and feel close to him.'

Ellen: 'I just pray about anything on my mind at the time, so that I can stop worrying about it and enjoy the service.'

Eileen: 'I like to be quiet. Sometimes I don't use any words at all. But I ask God to get me in the right mood.'

Terry: 'Oh! Hundreds of things — mainly about the worship and the message of it.'

Question 5

Patrick: 'Is it all right to pray to win a football match? Jesus did say we could ask anything.'

The trouble is, what's to stop the other side praying to win as well! Of course, you will tell God how much you want to win, but it seems more sensible to pray to be able to play as well as possible and to have strength to honour Jesus in victory or defeat. It is certainly right to pray about every part of our lives and to thank God for the enjoyment he gives us.

Question 6

Mandy: 'Is it all right for me to keep going to parties now that I am a Christian?

There's nothing wrong with the idea of parties. Jesus went to them. At least, we know of his presence at a wedding feast, and at gatherings of 'tax collectors and sinners'. People murmured: 'Look at him keeping such disreputable com-

pany!' But the important point is this: Jesus was never influenced for the bad, by the company he kept — they never dragged him down. In fact, he was helping many of them.

Instead of giving a definite yes or no, I suggest you ask yourself two questions:

1. *How strong a Christian are you?* In all honesty, do you think you will be dragged down by going to parties? Are you strong enough to trust in Jesus all the time, to do and say only what you know will please him? If so, go to them every so often and enjoy them. (It is important for Christians to mix with all sorts of non-Christians; how else will the others there have any contact with the Lord Jesus himself?) If not, it is wiser to steer clear, at least until you have grown up in your faith.

2. *What sort of party is it?* Some, of course, are utterly harmless — at worst, a waste of time and, at best, honest enjoyment of God's good gifts. However, it is at parties that people catch venereal disease and girls become pregnant. At parties, ordinary people are introduced to the world of drugs. At parties, alcohol flows freely and defences easily slip down. So try and weigh it all up first.

Question 7

Alfred: How much money should I put in the offering at church on Sunday?

Giving is one of the greatest joys for a Christian. The Bible assumes that, if you are a Christian, you will give. Your *attitude* to it is more important than the amount. Jesus said, 'Give first place to his (God's) kingdom,' and then he promises that, if you do this, you yourself won't go without. God's kingdom needs money which will only come if its members give it — after all, it really belongs to God, in any case. Give *regularly* (week by week) and give *cheerfully* (enjoying it) is how the Bible looks at the matter.

But, you will ask *'how much?'* The Old Testament required a tenth of people's income (ten per cent). This is still an excellent starting point. Say you earn £15 per week, then £1.50 is set aside straight away for God's work before you spend the rest. It may well be possible to give more; as a general rule we shouldn't give less. If you're a student, at school or college, and pocket money or grant make 10% an impossibility, fair enough, God understands. Work out what is the right proportion for you.

And remember, you owe some of this sum to your local church, but it is right also to give some to God's work overseas through his missionaries and those working to combat world hunger and other human needs.

Question 8

Vivien: 'I hear of people who claim that they are Christians and who hold seances. Is there anything wrong with this?'

Yes, there is! Spiritism (or the attempt to communicate with the spirits of those who have died) is becoming very popular. But it is definitely forbidden by God. (Read Leviticus 19.31 and 2 Samuel 28.7–25.) It is a temptation put in front of us by the devil who makes us strangely fascinated by it. We are to have nothing to do with it — for our sakes as much as God's — and a great deal of harm can come from dabbling in these matters (often called 'the occult'). If you are bothered by it, or in any way involved, go and get help — preferably from your minister.

Question 9

Christine: 'People say that God guides them. I don't think I've ever felt this. How does he guide?'

The Bible certainly talks of God guiding his people — at least those who were prepared to listen to his voice. The major thing, to start with, is to realize that God *wants* to guide you, then to pray for it, and then to *expect* it to happen.

He seems to speak to us in four main ways.

1 He uses what we might call *'sanctified common sense'*. The most sensible thing is usually God's will. If we stay close to him, and ask him to control our thoughts, we just need to work out the best way ahead. Often it is *after* a decision has been made that we can see that God has guided us. My wife and I have recently had to make a big decision about moving house and changing jobs. We didn't seem to have any clear leading from God and so we prayed like this: 'Lord, it seems right to take the new job, and if nothing happens before such and such a date, we will accept it. If this is wrong, please show us.' We took it — and can now see that God's hand was in it.

2 As we *read the Bible*, God speaks to us. Sometimes a sentence or a phrase will stand out, just as though it was written specially for us. We should expect God to speak personally to us.

3 *Christian friends* can be God's mouthpiece to us. It is a wise thing to ask advice — but beware of asking everyone you meet. That way, you will wait until you are told what you want to be told. Go for the advice of just one or two well-chosen friends.

4 God speaks to us through *things that happen*. If you keep failing your driving test, it is unlikely that he wants you to be a long-distance driver. If your father dies, it is likely that he wants you to find extra time and energy to be with and help your mother. It's back to the 'sanctified common sense' really.

These were real questions from one group of young Christians. What are yours? If you belong to a fellowship group, why not have a 'Name your hang-up' session and get an experienced Christian to come and answer your questions.

Something to do

ARE YOU KIDDING YOURSELF?

In the back streets, around where I live, hundreds of small boys, and some not so small, parade every evening in uniform. Not school uniform, not 'Brigade' uniform but *Manchester City* — and it's usually the 'away' strip for some mysterious reason. The boys are going through the motions of being stars and scoring goals. Then they punch the air above them for the benefit of the millions who will watch it on television later.

It's a marvellous world of make-believe, full of the magic of childhood. No one would deny it to them. But, things don't stay like this. The hard, real world will soon gobble them up. They'll discover soon enough that they aren't stars; most of them aren't even good at football. Certainly, they don't belong to Manchester City. Oh, yes, they wear the gear. They look the part. They do all the gestures better than the stars themselves. But they are not *really* professional footballers.

An amazing number of people are like this when it comes to the Christian life. As make-believe Christians, they go through the motions and try to do what Christians do. It's so easy to be like the boys in the streets; you can kid yourself all right. But, sooner or later, the hard truth will dawn; there's a *missing ingredient*.

It's like going to a disco during a power cut. Or you get hold of a car and fill the petrol tank with water. Try playing football without a ball. It's all the same: there's a vital *missing ingredient*.

For make-believe Christians, that ingredient is Jesus Christ himself. In the form of his Spirit, he lives within every Christian. If he is missing, no matter what you try to do — however much you go to church and help old ladies across the road — you are not really a Christian. You may succeed in kidding yourself, but there's one person you can't kid — and that is God.

This could just be your problem. If it is, this question should be yours too:

How can I become a truly committed Christian?

The answer goes something like this. You need to realize:

1 God loves you. He really wants you. We know this because he sent his Son, Jesus Christ, into the world to *find* us, to make us really *alive*.

2 It is your fault that you don't really know and experience God. It is because you don't really love him and you don't really love other people. Despite this fact — that you have sinned — God wants to forgive you. His Son died to make it possible.

If you can grasp these two things, it is really very simple. Just pray to God. Say sorry for going your own way and for not really loving him. And ask the Spirit of Jesus, alive again from the dead, to live in your life. You could use words something like these:

'Dear God. I am sorry I have drifted away from you. I have not really loved you. I have sinned. Thank you that you still love me and that your Son, Jesus Christ, died to save me from my sin. Come into my life, Holy Spirit of Jesus, and help me to live as you want me to.'

If you sincerely pray that, you can be sure that God will accept you.

One of Jesus' best-known stories is about two brothers and their father. The younger one had been a rebel and left home, but eventually he came back, genuinely sorry. This was cause for celebration, the father declared, for his son *'was dead, but now he is alive; he was lost, but now he has been found'*.

If you have said sorry to God and asked the Lord Jesus, by his Spirit, to come into your life, he will say the same of you.

You were *dead*. You were a dead person, wandering around trying to look alive. That's how the Father saw you. But when you came back home to him, you became *alive*.

You were *lost*, with no idea where life was taking you . . . no purpose, no meaning. But now, things are different — you are *found*.

If you happen to be in this position, if you are now really *alive* for the first time in your life, you have *started* on the best of all adventures. Don't keep it to yourself — tell someone else quickly and this will really help you.

It may be, however, that this short section doesn't answer your particular problem. Fair enough, but please don't give up. Tackle your minister or some other Christian whom you respect. There is an answer and it's well worth hunting for it. 'Seek and you will find,' said Jesus.

"God wants to forgive us"

Read the story for yourself. It is in Luke's Gospel, chapter 15, verses 11–32. Ask yourself (or discuss with others):
1 In what way is God like the father in the story?
2 Are *you* kidding yourself like the elder son and thinking that all is well between you and the Father?
3 How could the younger son be *sure* that his father had accepted and forgiven him?

Things to think further about

ALONE WITH GOD

Are you a 'labour savour'? You can cook a meal in three minutes, thanks to tins and packets. Your washing, drying and airing can all be done automatically as long as you know how to press the right knobs. You can (if the advertisements can be believed) learn a language in a fortnight if you just buy a record. Cut out the time, cut out the slog, be an 'instant person'.

But can the things that matter be achieved just like that? Like being skilled at your job, or an artist, or even a *friend*?

Being a Christian is all about being friends. Friends with God. And a friendship takes time to build up. You can't enjoy the special 'togetherness' of a close friendship if you are never together. So it makes sense to get together with God sometimes — not as a duty but to enjoy his friendship.

There are no short-cuts, no easy labour-saving ways of going places in your Christian life. You can't be an instant mature Christian. But just as a craftsman doesn't find that all the hours put into learning his skills are boring, and a professional pop group revels in continual practice, so the Christian really can enjoy getting together with God and growing up as a result. We all find that it goes up and down — sometimes being alone with God is great, sometimes disappointing. But my experience has been that overall it's well worth it — a must.

Young Christians often ask this simple question: *'How long ought I to spend alone with God*? There's no set answer. The late Martin Luther-King was often away from home in the cause of his Civil Rights Movement in America, and he saw little of his children. But when he was with them, he gave them all his attention. 'It's not quantity of time, but quality that matters,' he used to say. Our relationship with God is just the same: two minutes really enjoying his closeness is much better than a boring hour of wandering thoughts. Start small — say 7 minutes — *and aim for it to grow bigger*.

Two other basic questions are 'When?' and 'How?'

1 When should I get alone with God?

We had an interesting discussion about this with our young people and I started it by asking them if they had regular times alone with God and, if so, when?

Syd: (Car parts salesman) 'No, I don't — not really.'

Kevin: (Gardener) 'I do — in the morning before work. I

get gotten up by my mum. I often do it without realizing what I'm doing — but it's a good habit, really.'

Syd: 'I've got four speakers off my record player and I sit in the middle of my bed with my Bible — it's really immaculate — and I just sit there with the thing at about half volume and I just turn my ears off and I think. It's ridiculous!'

Lynn: (Income tax worker) 'I find at night it's lovely because it's quiet and dead peaceful and I'm sitting up in bed. If I lie down I've got no chance — I'm off to sleep. If that starts to happen I have to get out and kneel beside my bed.'

Kevin: 'I feel guilty if I stay in bed.'

Ruth: (Nursery nursing trainee) 'The trouble is my bedroom is so cold. I read my Bible and pray at night, except when I'm on holiday and then I do it in the middle of the day. I like to swop over and do something different sometimes — when I was doing exams, I did it in the morning.'

Christine: (Office worker) 'I'm never awake in the morning!'

So it went on. No one necessarily any better than the others, but all different. A regular habit and variety are both good. Do what seems best for you. Try to be alone and undisturbed (even if you're like Syd and you need noise to concentrate!). And remember, *it's God you're really meeting with.*

2 How do I have a time alone with God?

Like any friendship, the great thing about it is just being together. We don't have to talk all the time. Part of it is listening, anyway, as God speaks to us.

Let God speak to you.

He does this in different ways — through what you hear, read, think, feel, etc. A favourite way of his for speaking to us is through the *Bible*, which calls itself '*God's Word*'.

It's a good idea to read only a few verses of the Bible and to read them two or three times, looking out for particular things God wants to say to you. What can I learn about God? Is there an example here? Or a warning? A promise? A command? Something meant for *me*? And it's important, before you read, to pray something like this: 'Lord, I'm listening. What are you saying to me today?' And after you've read, pray about what you have learnt and ask for help in remembering it and putting it into practice.

My wife and I use *Daily Bread*, some Bible reading notes produced by Scripture Union. I've been using them for over ten years and still find them helpful. Apart from helping us to understand what we read, the notes take us through the whole Bible in about five years. If you don't use any notes, you tend always to read your favourite bits of the Bible and don't get a balanced diet.

You speak to God.

It's helpful to have three different kinds of things to say:

Thank you. There's no limit to this. Just stop and think of all you have to be grateful for. Then look at God himself and praise and thank him for all he is and all he has done.

Sorry. It's sad, but we have to keep saying sorry to God. But the Psalms say, 'If I had ignored my sins, the Lord would not have listened to me.' (Psalm 66.18)

Please. The Lord Jesus said, 'Ask and you will receive' (Matthew 7.7). We need to ask for many, many things — the day ahead, our family and friends . . . Why not make a list to help you remember who and what to pray for?

Talking to God in prayer comes with practice. Be natural. You haven't got to use special language or anything like that, but if it helps, do use a book of written-out prayers. Try to link what you have learnt from the Bible with your prayers.

Sample Prayer List

Sunday	Mum / Vicar and family / All preaching today
Monday	Dad / Work - those at work
Tuesday	Our Kenny / The Youth Club / Phil and Dorothy in S. America
Wednesday	Our Beryl / Girl friend(s)!
Thursday	Gran / The Bible Study
Friday	Aunt Gertrude / All old people
Saturday	The whole family / Safety on roads / Things on my mind.

Things to think and talk about

1 What do you think is the best time of the day to be 'alone with God'?
2 Do you believe Syd (page 31) when he says he needs noise to concentrate on God properly?
3 Read Matthew 7.7–11. What do you think Jesus meant?

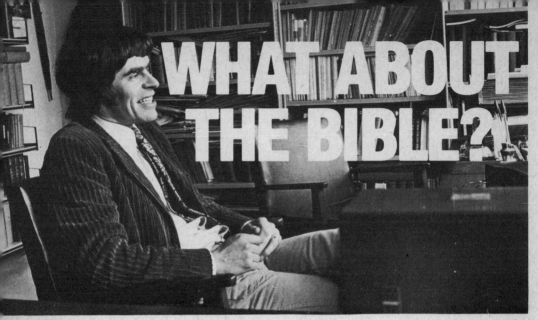

WHAT ABOUT THE BIBLE?

I thought I'd dig out someone who knew what he was talking about. You can't believe what any old person says about the Bible. So, with fear and trepidation, I took my tape recorder round one afternoon to Manchester University to find a *Professor*, no less.

I needn't have been so frightened. Professor F. F. Bruce, one of the leading New Testament scholars in the country, was friendly, human and very humble.

Once we got going, this was how our conversation went:

CF   Professor Bruce, how long have you been studying the Bible?

FFB   More or less, since I began to read, for my parents encouraged me to read the Bible. I guess I've been a Bible student for nearly sixty years.

CF   Why have you given your life to a study of the Bible?

FFB   Because I have always found it the most interesting body of literature in the world.

CF   What is so special about the Bible when you compare it with other literature?

FFB   The fact that the Bible is always relevant, I should think. Reading the Bible is like holding up a mirror to human life today — personal life, social and international life as well. Time and time again, one finds in reading the Bible that there is a message that directly speaks to the situation that we are living through.

CF   What is the Bible?

FFB   The Bible, at its highest level, is the record of the way in which God has made himself known to mankind. This, of course, has found its climax in Jesus Christ.

CF   Why should we believe the Bible?

FFB   We can test its truth on two levels. We can test it *historically*, just as we should test the historical accuracy of any other work. It stands up very well to these tests. For instance, we look at all we know about the Roman Empire at the time when Jesus lived and the apostles taught. Then we can fit the New Testament writings into their historical setting and see how perfectly they fit there.

But the Bible has to be tested at a level which is higher than the historical: *personally*. What does this matter to me? For instance, if it says that through faith in Christ I may enjoy peace with God, a sense of my sins being forgiven, I can only test the truth of these claims by putting my faith in Christ.

CF   And you would say that on both of these levels you have discovered that the Bible certainly is reliable?

FFB   Indeed, yes.

CF   How did the Bible come into being?

FFB   Over a period of many centuries. The early part of the Bible, the Old Testament writings, took something like 1,000 years to reach their final shape. They record the history of God's dealings particularly with one nation, the nation of Israel, in which, in due course, Jesus Christ was born. The New Testament is simply the record of how Christ came, what he did, what he taught, how he died, how he triumphed, and the beginnings of the Christian movement which was launched as a result.

CF   How important a part should the Bible play in the life of a Christian?

FFB   A very important part. The Bible, above everything else, is the witness to Christ and, in order to have our lives shaped by Christ, we need to study the Bible.

We belong to the 'open' generation. We've lost the old embarrassment of talking about sex quite openly. Even death can be discussed. But mention Jesus Christ, and people feel uneasy. If you are challenged about your faith in Christ, you'll be tempted to change the subject.

It's thoroughly healthy that the name of Jesus doesn't come lightly to our lips, that we have to think before mentioning him. It's a terrible thing to lose this respect which he always deserves. But it is quite another matter to be *ashamed* of him, to be *afraid* to talk about him. Don't get the idea that we can be secret Christians. We have to be willing to speak up for Jesus Christ. He said so in no uncertain terms:

'If a person is ashamed of me and of my teaching in this godless and wicked day, then the Son of Man will be ashamed of him when he comes in the glory of his Father with the holy angels.' (Mark 8.38)

During winter, the St. Lawrence River in Canada gets completely frozen at the mouth. Someone has said that many Christians have this same problem — they are 'frozen at the mouth'. If it's your problem too, confess it to God and ask him

GOOD NEWS TO SHARE

to melt your mouth and give you an opportunity to speak for him. Then, look out for this opportunity — it may come really soon. When it does, take it and you'll discover a tremendous excitement.

Soon after I became a committed Christian, I was asked to go to a church to explain briefly during the service what my faith meant to me. I went along petrified. In due course, I was shown up into a high pulpit and, just as I was opening my mouth, someone switched a tape-recorder on. If ever I wanted to disappear, it was then. I prayed desperately — 'Lord, please give me the words.' I don't remember now what I did say. But I do remember the feeling of amazement and elation that I had straight afterwards. God had given me the

words to say. He had used *me*, although I felt so inadequate. (I know now it was *because* I felt inadequate in my own strength.)

As Christians, then, it's our responsibility and, in many ways, our greatest thrill to share our faith in Jesus Christ with others. But, two questions arise:

1 How on earth do I get the conversation round to God?

This bothers a lot of Christians. The answer is that you haven't always got to be trying to twist the conversation round. If you ask God to give you opportunities and then look out for them, you can be sure they will come, sooner or later. Perhaps a friend will ask you a question that puts you on the spot. They might ask you what you did last night, for instance, the day after you went to a Bible study. Or perhaps people are discussing a television programme about flying saucers, a monastery, or even an investigation into the claims of Christ.

This sort of opportunity crops up constantly — just look out for it and cash in on it. People may well be intrigued if you have something positive and definite to say (as long as it's in normal, everyday language and said quite naturally). You can spot anyone who is genuinely interested and try to take things further with that particular person.

"God gives opportunities"

2 What should I say if someone really is interested?

There are, of course, many different ways of speaking for Jesus. But, it may help to realize that there are two kinds of things to say about the Gospel. (By the way, Gospel means quite simply 'good news'.)

(a) *The facts of the Gospel*. Yes, Christianity *is* based on facts, real events of history.

(b) *Our experience of the Gospel* — what Jesus Christ means to us, here and now.

We need both facts and experience. Emphasize the facts only and it will be dry and unreal — just like a boring history lesson. 'So what?' people may say. Emphasize the experience only and the reply will come — 'That's O.K. for you, but I'm different.'

The facts of the Gospel

About God

He is our Maker.
He loves us.
He is holy and cannot bear sin.

About Jesus Christ

He really existed.
He was (and is) the Son of God.
He shows us what God is like.
He died for our sins.
He rose again.
He offers *eternal life* (something which begins here and now).

We have all sinned against God.
We need God's forgiveness.
We can only have this forgiveness and eternal life if we believe in Jesus Christ. (This means *trusting* him personally.)

You won't tell everyone all of these things, but they are most of the facts that people need to grasp in order to become Christians. Some people become Christians, of course, when they still know very little.

Our experience of the Gospel

A sample 'testimony' by Mary from Wickham Market, Suffolk.

'I heard about Christianity at our Church Youth Fellowship but had brushed it aside as something I couldn't believe in. I think I didn't want to believe it, because I couldn't come up to the standards that would be expected of me.

Anyway, I went on a Youth Fellowship holiday to the Isle of Man in 1972. Every night of the holiday, we had *Focus* meetings, where leaders gave talks about Jesus. I thought these were pretty harmless until one night my friend told me that one of the talks had made her think. I was angry about this — now I know it was the devil telling me it was wrong.

The next night, I promised myself I wouldn't listen. It was so quiet, as if everyone was concentrating, and so I opened my Bible and read Leviticus — I thought if anything could put me off, that would! At the end of the meeting, the speaker said a prayer. During it, I kept saying the verse 'Mary had a little lamb' to stop myself from listening, but I found myself saying 'Jesus had a little lamb'. If that wasn't bad enough, two of my friends stayed behind because they wanted to become Christians.

Again, I was angry, because they'd got something I didn't think I could have. I couldn't understand why I wasn't happy and kept trying to avoid all the Christians. I think I went to bed earlier than anyone that night, but I couldn't sleep. The inevitable happened; our leader, Sonia, from Wickham Market, came and talked to me. I was tense and had a knotted feeling inside me, from fighting the devil. Finally, with all my heart, I prayed a prayer and asked the Lord to come into my life and fill me and forgive all my sins.

After that, I felt so relaxed and happy. I couldn't think why I hadn't done it earlier.

But it wasn't a complete bed of roses and after the holiday, when there wasn't as much fellowship, it was difficult. Things did get a bit rocky, but I've found that we're always lifted up by the Lord and I've proved that Christianity works.

Jesus has given me a different attitude to so many things. I find I appreciate much more everything around me. And now I find it easier to see the good in people rather than always criticizing. At school, he makes a real difference, especially when things aren't going well. I'm hopeless at maths but if I pray about it, he really helps me.'

These are the kind of things which we will want to share with our friends. *'But I could never remember all that — this isn't for me,'* some will say. Fair enough; you probably won't remember it all. But it *is* for you.

Jesus once healed a blind man and this caused a great stir. The religious leaders wanted to know who had done it, and they pestered the poor fellow. He didn't know much about Jesus, but 'one thing I do know', he said. 'I was blind and now I see.' You can do that; tell what you *do* know of Christ. As you get into the swing of it, you'll soon learn more.

Steve is better than a railway time-table. He always knows the time of any train you want. Someone once asked him how he did it. 'It's easy — by using train-times all the time,' he replied. (He works on the railways.) It's the same with the Gospel and useful bits of the Bible — you soon get to know them if you are often talking about them — if you are often *using* them. Steve is a Christian and once he pointed this out — 'the more we do it, the more we learn'.

One night at *Open House* (our Youth Club), Jimmy came up to me, cigarette in mouth, surrounded by noisy friends and amidst the blare of pop music and the pounding of footballs on the wall next door. He asked me a question which no one had ever asked me before: *'I want to become a Christian. What have I got to do?'*

His broad Scottish accent makes Jimmy hard for us in Manchester to understand. So I twice asked him to repeat his question. Yes, I had heard it right. He wasn't drunk. He seemed to be sincere and so I had to take his request seriously.

I told him the four steps that had helped me several years previously. Despite all the noise and the presence of his curious friends, Jimmy listened carefully as we went through the ABCD.

A   Admit your sin. We have all sinned against God. Sin cuts us off from friendship with him. So, we have to admit this to God and say that we are sorry. (Jimmy read out the two verses from the Bible which I found: Romans 3.23 and Romans 6.23.)

B   Believe that Jesus died for you. Although we deserve death because of our sin, God gave his Son for us. He died so that we could live. He went through it for us; by this he has done everything and we can't do anything ourselves to make God accept us. (We looked up Romans 5.8 because it was near to the previous verses, but 1 Peter 3.18 would be even clearer.)

C   Count the cost. It won't be easy. Jesus never said it would be. It will involve trying to please him in every department of life. We will have to admit to being a Christian and, with God's help, give up what we know is wrong. (We looked up Luke 9.23. I expected that Jimmy would give up at this point. But no, 'I can face that,' he said.)

D   Do something. Imagine Jesus knocking at a door — the door of your life. He invites you to let him in. 'If anyone hears my voice and opens the door, I will come into his house and eat with him,' he says. (Revelation 3.20) A small, simple step — but one which revolutionizes your life, turns it upside down or, rather, turns it the right way up. Jesus Christ, by his Holy Spirit (known as the Spirit of Jesus) promises to enter your life, if invited.

"A revolutionary step"

Jimmy could hardly wait to pray a prayer asking Jesus to come into his life. So, down in the club, in front of his mates, he prayed out loud. I suggested he should go and tell someone else what had happened to him. He told Joey — the toughest fellow he could have found. Joey hit him straight in the face. I was staggered, but even more so when Jimmy offered his other cheek — only to have that struck as well!

As you will have gathered, Jimmy's story is unusual. People don't usually appear out of the blue asking how to become Christians. As a rule, it takes a long time to win someone for Christ.

It depends on patiently loving him or her in the way that Jesus does, spending time together, knowing him or her as a real friend.

It depends on praying faithfully for your friend.

It depends on showing a real Christian example in your life.

You probably won't have to do it all anyway. At some stage, you may well be able to introduce your friend to a Christian group, like your Youth Fellowship or Christian Union, a Gospel Concert — or even a church service. These can help. But the vital work is your own personal sharing of your faith. So, remember the ABCD — there is no thrill, no excitement like that of leading someone to Jesus Christ. I

will always remember Jimmy, that's for sure.

Here are a few more questions which may have been going through your mind and a few answers which I hope don't sound too glib:—

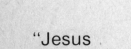

"Jesus reveals God"

What if people ask difficult questions?

This may well happen. Try to spot how serious it is — it may be an attempt to distract you. If not, do your best to answer it. Don't be afraid to admit you don't know the answer; just go and get help from a more experienced Christian.

Why should I believe that God exists?

When this is asked, you can humbly suggest that it takes more faith to believe that there *isn't* a God than that there *is* one. Point to the vastness of the universe, the wonders of the world of nature, and, especially, the most amazing of all creation — *man himself*. Did they all just happen? Is there no master designer behind them all?

Then you can point to *Jesus Christ*. He is the one who really shows us that there is a God.

But Jesus was just a good man. Why do you say that he was God?

Surely he was like no other man. If he wasn't God, he must have been either a liar or a madman, either deceiving others or deceived himself.

Look at his *life*. Surely, if he had ever done anything wrong, someone would have 'let on'. But no-one, neither his friends (like Peter and John), nor his enemies (like the religious leaders), nor those who were neutral (like Pontius Pilate), found any fault at all with him.

Look at his *claims*. He acted and spoke as God. He forgave sins. He said, 'I and the Father are one.'

Look especially at his *resurrection*. Jesus had died and his followers were lost and scared. Yet, within a few weeks, they were going everywhere preaching about Jesus and his resurrection. People have tried to disprove it — but it can't be done!

Face Jesus Christ honestly and you'll see that he was the Son of God.

I believe in God — surely that's enough?

Jesus didn't think so. All those who came into conflict with him still believed in God. You see, there are two kinds of belief:

(i) intellectual — in the head only. Even the Devil believes in God in this way.

(ii) practical — affecting our whole life. The best word for this is *trust*.

So, when a Christian is described as someone who believes in Jesus Christ, it means trusting him personally and not just believing in your head that he exists.

Why does God allow so much suffering?

This is a very big and very difficult subject. We have to admit that we don't really know the answer. But much suffering can, in some way, be traced to man's greed, selfishness, pride or stupidity. If not, we have to say that we live in a less than perfect world; the Bible traces this back to the first entry of sin into this world.

Ask a Christian who has suffered; he won't understand it. But he will almost certainly say that God has been incredibly real throughout it and he has learnt a lot because of it.

Why does God allow Hell if he loves us?

The answer is simply that:

(i) He has given us free-will and this obviously includes freedom to do wrong.

(ii) He is utterly pure and holy. He cannot, by his nature, put up with sin. This may not be what we think we'd be like if we were God — but we're not! Because of our wrong, we condemn ourselves to Hell, unless we take note that . . .

(iii) God has provided the only way out of Hell in Jesus Christ.

If I became a Christian, how could I possibly keep it up?

You can't possibly keep it up in your own strength. But God gives his Holy Spirit — with all his power — to those who become Christians.

It is just necessary for you to *want* to be kept going by him.

Why can't I wait until I'm old before becoming a Christian?

A dangerous attitude! What makes you think you'll last that long?

1 What excuses do you tend to give for not sharing your faith with others?
2 Do you think that wearing a badge or sticker is a help or hindrance?
3 In what ways can we put people off Christianity if we are not careful?
4 What are the main things which stop people from becoming Christians?

Things to talk or think about

FAILURE

Ever felt a failure? Like the rare occasion when you do the washing up for Mum and you break one of her cups. Or you go into school without having done your homework. Or your boss tells you your work is shoddy.

Failure is every Christian's problem. God wants us to be like Jesus. Perhaps *we* want to be like Jesus. And we're not. The Bible's word for this is sin — an unpopular word today, but a good straightforward word. Sin has to be faced, not explained away.

A group of young people were discussing sin one Sunday night, after church. Some of the things they said have sparked off this section of the book.

Lynn: 'I never thought of sin as a thing like shouting at someone. I didn't realize sin was so real and not just committing adultery or murdering someone. You need forgiveness for so many things.'
Christine: 'Well, what is sin, anyway?'

What is sin?

Sin is breaking God's laws. Jesus summed these laws up like this:

1. *Love the Lord your God* with all your heart, your mind, your soul and your strength.

2. *Love your neighbour* as yourself.

So anything which doesn't measure up to this standard is sin. It can be what we do and what we don't do. It can be our thoughts and it can be our words. It affects every single one of us.

I'm writing this while I'm in bed with flu. I keep wanting to get up. I tell myself I'm all right — it's all in the mind. So I get out of bed — and my head spins all over the place. I've got to face the fact that I've got flu and I must set about getting better. Like staying in bed, taking my pills, waiting . . . .

We've all got the sin bug. We're made that way. And Jesus is the only cure, a daily cure.

Pete: 'I had terrible guilt feelings a lot . . . I didn't feel confident enough that I could come back to God every time.'

Should a Christian still have guilt feelings?

No.
Why not?

When Jesus died for you, he took all your guilt on himself. You remember his shout of agony: 'My God, my God, why have you forsaken me?' At that moment he was suffering all the consequences of your sin and my sin, past sin and future sin. Our shame had become his. Our death had become his. Our guilt had become his. Then, as he was on the point of dying, he let out the greatest victory cry of all time — 'It is finished!'

He had done everything that could be done. He had exchanged places with you. He had exchanged places with you. You can be free. Everyone can be free. This is how the most famous verse in the Bible puts it: 'God loved the world so much that he gave his only Son, so that everyone who believes in him may not die but have eternal life'. (John 3.16)

God isn't trying to catch you out. He wants you. He loves you. He accepts you — *as you are*. Just believe in him and what his word says. That's all you have to do, that's all you *can* do. Let him take away all the guilt — get on with living as a free person, for him.

Christine: 'I think I took it for granted when I first started out that I'd be forgiven. I thought – well it doesn't matter what I do because if I say I'm sorry, it's all forgotten.'

Does it matter if a Christian goes on sinning?

Christine, picture the perfect boyfriend — or, even better, your future husband. You really love him; he really loves you. Even if you do something to upset him, you know he'll forgive you because you know he loves you.

So does it matter if you hurt him? Does it matter if you slap him in the face, if you say cruel things about him, or if you flirt with another boy? Of course it does. It's bound to spoil your relationship with him. If it continues, it will prove something too: you don't love him after all.

If you love Jesus, it's just the same. You don't go on hurting him by sinning — it doesn't make sense. Sin really does hurt him.

Kevin: 'The trouble is that sin is so powerful and it's so attractive. You know you shouldn't but it seems impossible to stop it.'

How can I stop sinning?

In your own strength, you can't. Temptation is very great, and remember, it's not wrong to be tempted, only to give way to the temptation. Whenever you're tempted, there are two choices: either you give in, or you do (or say, or think) something else.

Jesus called sin 'darkness' and himself 'light'. If you don't want to go into the dark, you've to stay where it's light.

'I am the light of the world,' he said. 'Whoever follows me will have the light of life and will never walk in darkness.' (John 8.12) How do you 'follow' Jesus? It's really a matter of *thinking* about him a lot and telling him about your temptations. The battle is usually in your mind. Think all the time about the temptation, and the battle is as good as lost. Think about Jesus and his Spirit is at your disposal to win the battle for you.

Make no mistake — *battle* is the right word for it. *Pete* has a particular kind of temptation: DRUGS. Once you've taken drugs, their pull is fantastically strong. It was while in prison that Pete became a Christian. He's out of prison now and a notable member of Platters, our Youth Fellowship. But the temptation to go back to his old mates, and to get 'high', is always with him.

If he keeps thinking about it, he doesn't stand a chance — it's so easy to go back to drugs. And he's done so more than once. His only hope is to fix his thoughts on Jesus and claim the power of his Spirit.

Sadly, we do all fall sometimes. When we do, the best thing is to say sorry to God straight away and accept his amazing forgiveness. Then ask yourself what lesson you've learnt from it.

As we grow up in our Christian lives, we become more (not less) aware of sin. The more like Jesus we are, the more we hate sin.

Things to think and talk about

1 Think of times when you've given way to temptation. What lessons can you learn from these times?
2 Why do you think that the word 'sin' is unpopular today?
3 Try to express in your own words all that the death of Jesus did for you.

Sin is

. . . not loving God most of all . . . being pleased with myself . . .

coming short of God's standards . . .

. . . pretending to be what I'm not . . .

. . . not being a loving sort of person.

WHAT ABOUT SEX?

Q Does God approve of sex?

A   Yes. It's a gift from God and, like all his gifts, it is very good and meant to be enjoyed. But — just like our money, our time and our abilities — our sexuality is to be used and enjoyed in the way God has laid down. Provided that we do that and don't play around with it, God is in favour of sex — and so can we be. (By the way, some people say that all sin is to do with sex — it isn't!) But, as you will have discovered, sex can be very powerful and needs to be under God's control.

Q It seems that Christians disapprove of sex outside marriage, but they can't say why. Why should we wait until marriage?

A   God designed and made us. Therefore, he knows — much better than we do — how our bodies and minds are supposed to function. He makes it clear in his word (the Bible) that sexual intercourse is for marriage, and for marriage only. This is how God described marriage right at the beginning of creation:

'A man will leave his father and mother and unite with his wife, and the two will become one.' (Genesis 2.24) Sex is seen as tremendously important: it sets the seal on two people being deeply united together. And this is only possible within a marriage relationship. So, for the Christian, *it is simply a question of admitting 'God knows best'.*

But, even if you are not a Christian, I believe that common sense also says: 'Wait until marriage'.

(i) A deep sexual relationship must be part of a *secure* relationship (otherwise one or both partners — usually the girl — are unable to give themselves fully).

(ii) If you sleep together and then break off your relationship, you either regret it or else you cheapen sex.

(iii) Waiting never did anyone any harm.

(iv) Waiting teaches you respect and trust for one another: a vital part of a good sex relationship.

Tony and Ellen are a young couple who met as students and got married. A year or so later, they became Christians. The other day, they were speaking frankly about the way this had changed their outlook on sex.

Tony: 'We slept together regularly before we got married — I suppose lots of couples do. But it built up a real tension for us, a real sense of guilt.'

Ellen: 'Obviously, now we're Christians, we wish we had waited until we were married. I don't think we would have lost anything by waiting. But, we know God has forgiven us and doesn't hold it against us.'

Tony: 'I think sex is now more important, more meaning-ful in a way . . .'

Q   I am fifteen and enjoy going out with boys. There's nothing wrong with this, is there?

A   It's very healthy and right to enjoy being with mem-bers of the opposite sex. A friendship *under God's direction and control* can be a real help. Trust the Lord and obey him.

But, when you narrow the field down to one boy friend, there are dangers. Provided you don't actually do anything wrong, there's no harm in it at all — but it can be a *hindrance* to your Christian life.

(i) You can easily be distracted from serving God and trying to get to know him better.

(ii) Just because 'everyone has a boy friend', it doesn't mean God wants you to.

(iii) If he's not a Christian, you will certainly slip in your Christian life. It's like you standing on a table, him on the floor — it's hard to pull him up but easy for him to pull you down.

Q   I seem to have feelings for members of my own sex all the time. Am I 'queer'? If so, what should I do?

A   This is a possibility, due to a lack of balance in your hormones. A doctor tells me that most of us are capable of homosexual feelings, and also capable of controlling these feelings as we mix with the opposite sex. However, if this is a big problem for you, don't keep it to yourself. Consult your doctor and your minister. And remember — God knows and understands. Confide in him and seek his strength.

"God understands"

Q   Is it wrong to enjoy sex by yourself?

A   This is called masturbation. For many boys and girls, it's a normal part of growing up and discovering our-selves. Dr. Charles W. Schedd says in his entertaining and helpful book *The Stork is Dead,* that he taught his children that it was a 'gift of God', but also a part of 'growing up', a phase, not something to get stuck with. Not all Christians would agree with this view, but certainly, as Dr. Schedd says, 'Teenage masturbation is preferable to teenage intercourse.' With so much sex thrown at us today, the pressures can be enormous, and here can be the means of release.

But beware — it can be an escape into the world of fantasy; you can depend on imaginary relationships which you'd be ashamed to admit. Ask God constantly to keep your thoughts clean and help you to have *real* relationships with people.

Q The fellows at work are always bringing in magazines full of photos of nudes. What should my attitude be?

A First, realize that it is natural to long to look at them. God designed the female body and he did a good job. But, just looking at sexy pictures can never satisfy anyone. It arouses you unnecessarily. It helps to cut sex off from love and relationships, and it degrades the female sex. If you have an overwhelming desire to look at these magazines, you're probably in male company too much! Get to know *real* girls and enjoy their company.

However, don't look down on your workmates. If, with Jesus' help, you don't look at the magazines, they'll respect you (even if they laugh at first). You may even get a chance to have a good talk about 'What's the point of them, anyway?' Which could lead on to talking about your standards in life (that is God's standards) and the power God gives to keep them.

"God's standards are our standards"

Q I like dressing sexily and can't see anything wrong in it. Can you?

A If you said attractively, I would agree with you. But sexily? It sounds as though your aim at least is to stimulate boys, if not actually to catch your prey. Does that sound a reason which is worthy of a follower of Jesus? You may not realize just how easily you delicious females turn us helpless males on. You must be fair. Be attractive, be fashionable, but not provocative. 'Modesty' is the good old-fashioned word for it. Simon Peter was married — and his words about beauty are worth thinking about. He said you do not have to depend on 'outward aids' to make yourselves beautiful. 'Instead, your beauty should consist of your true, inner self, the ageless beauty of a gentle and quiet spirit, which is of the greatest value in God's sight.' (1 Peter 3.3,4)

Q What is the point of a marriage service? Surely it's enough just to decide to live together?

A In theory, you are right. The Bible certainly regards sleeping together as making you married in God's eyes. But the trouble is, we're human beings and sinful. Marriage is being undermined today and broken homes are a terrible tragedy — it's the children who suffer. So, anything which increases a sense of permanence and security in a marriage is a good thing. Just because both partners are Christians, it doesn't guarantee a successful marriage; Christians can give way to temptation, too.

So, the making of vows before God, in the presence of your family and friends, makes the commitment to each other much more meaningful and binding. The service as a whole, enables you to start out on a great adventure, with the prayers of many people to support you.

Q   My boy friend and I are about to get engaged. How far should I let him go with me?

A   This is hard to answer. I'm glad you word it as you do because, although both of you must act responsibly, the girl usually finds it easier to put the brakes on. Almost certainly you ought to go slower than both of you want. Somebody once said that you should say to your loved one, 'Go slowly, my love, and see all the fine things there are in me. Go fast, and I shall see how little there is in you.' Easier said than done, but it's possible — with God's help. The ideal is to 'pace' things carefully so that *gradually* you go further with each other. And, by the time you reach your wedding night, the natural next stage is full sexual intercourse. But remember —

(i) Christian standards are different from those of many non-Christians. It's necessary to make a definite stand, or you'll slip, too.

(ii) Once you've started being intimate in a particular way (from holding hands right on to 'heavy petting'), it's very, very hard to stop. We naturally want to go one step further — discipline is needed!

Q   I can hardly believe that God has given me such a gorgeous girl. How can I be sure she's right for me?

A   So you've discovered that God isn't a spoil-sport. Great! I assume that your thoughts are turning to the possibility of marriage. Here are some tests you could apply:—

Inclusive/Exclusive test. Are we able to share our friendship with others, or are we always hiving off on our own? If we can mix — all right. If we've just been selfish — together all the time — it's been unhealthy. But this is something that can be put right.

Friendship test. Are we really good friends (not just turned-on physically)? 'Will she still love me when I'm 65?'

Respect test. Would I like her to be the mother of my children?

Sharing test. Do we naturally want to *share everything*? Are we able to share faith in the Lord Jesus and pray together? If not, scrap ideas of marriage; God forbids Christians to marry non-Christians. (See 1 Corinthians 6.14,15)

Peace of mind test. Are we both deeply happy that the relationship is God's will? God tells us if something is wrong by making us feel uneasy — by taking away our peace of mind.

"God isn't a spoil-sport"

YOU'RE A CHRISTIAN AT WORK, TOO

You probably spend more of your waking hours at work than anywhere else.

God intends us to work — he made us that way. But because we live in a less than perfect world, our work is less than perfect and so, often, is the satisfaction we get from it. But, because it is God's will for us, we have to take our work seriously.

Work is so different for different people. It's one of the amazing things about the human race that we are so varied. Imagine what a problem we'd have if no one was cut out to be a dustman . . . or a politician . . . or a farmhand. As a clergyman, a lot of people think I don't know what work is! Although twelve to fourteen hours a day, six days a week, seems to be the order of the day, my problems and pressures are certainly different from those of many other people. But, for all Christians, no matter what job we find ourselves doing, *we are still Christians at work*. It is not possible to leave our Christianity behind and save it for home or church.

A variety of jobs are done by members of our Youth Fellowship but I was surprised to discover, when we were talking together one evening, how similar many of their problems were. Some were fortunate enough really to enjoy their work, but by no means all.

I don't really enjoy my work

Take Mike, for instance. Poor chap, he has to admit to being an income tax clerk! 'The work's a bit boring,' he says. 'It tends to be rather impersonal, you know; it's all numbers,

"Somebody's got to do this job"

figures and phone calls. To be honest, it's not interesting work, but I look at it like this — somebody's got to do it and it's just a job, really.'

It's good that Mike has come to see it that way. We work to be useful and to earn our keep, as well as to find satisfaction. Not all jobs are satisfying, by any means, but whatever we do, we can at least do it as well as possible, working for God as well as for our employer.

My workmates are the biggest problem

That is what most of the young people say. Those they work with often have very different standards from the Christian ones which they are trying to follow. Life would be so much easier (we like to think) if we could work only with Christians. But we have to rub shoulders with non-Christians. Jesus, praying to his Father, said this about it: 'They (my followers) do not belong to the world, just as I do not belong to the world. I do not ask you to take them out of the world, but I do ask you to keep them safe from the Evil One.' (John 17.14, 15)

What was Jesus thinking of when he said we need 'keeping safe'? Could it be the sort of things Derek, George, Laura and Christine find at work?

Derek works in a big warehouse as a pattern maker and he finds his workmates tough. 'They're always swearing,' he says: 'Every other word is "f——" and they sort of point you out if you don't swear as though you're a freak or something. They're all gamblers, on the horses every afternoon, and they go boozing at dinner time.'

George, a sewerage labourer, agrees with Derek. He

finds it just the same: 'It's really difficult to keep out of their ways.'

If you find that you need to follow a different way of life in order to please God, it takes courage and it needs praying about. It's a challenge: are you prepared to be different?

Girls have similar problems, of course. *Laura* works in an office of a big department store. Because she goes to a weekly Christian meeting in her dinner break, she finds that people call her names and do their best to drag her down.

Christine admits to a different problem in the office where she works. 'It's the men!' she says, with a glint in her eye, showing that part of her enjoys the problem. 'Most of them are married but they keep coming up and putting their arms round you and trying to get close to you.'

This is a typical office temptation. The man, away from his home life, which is often a bit stale anyway, fancies some excitement with an attractive girl. The girl is flattered by his attention and eggs him on. She doesn't think about the consequences. And Christians find the temptation just as real as non-Christians do. It calls for sticking close to the Lord Jesus and remembering his standards: faithfulness in marriage, keeping sex just for marriage and respecting other people (not using them).

I think I'll have to change jobs

Workmates certainly can and do cause problems — but they are not impossible to cope with. If, however, you find you can't live a Christian life at work because of the pressure your mates put on you, you are probably in the wrong job. Perhaps you should look around for something else, but don't rush into doing this. Young people tend to give up a job too easily and sometimes for the wrong reasons. It is *not* a good idea to change jobs often. Only do so when you're sure it's right.

It's easy to be dishonest

On the question of honesty, the young people had to be prodded into talking. *Gordon*, however, was forthcoming. He works in a bank and has to fill in a time-sheet to show his hours at work. 'If you're a quarter of an hour late coming in, you find yourself still wanting to put nine o'clock down. And, when you do overtime, it isn't really checked what time you leave, so you could put down any time.'

Jane has a phone where she works and is tempted to use it for her own private calls whenever she likes. Others find different things to steal from the firm: time, equipment (like stationery and pens), etc.

Obviously, God wants his people to be honest, but Jesus told us to be 'wise as serpents'. If you get all your workmates in the soup by your honesty to the boss, you're more than likely clumsy as a bull. It would be better to have it out with your mates first. If your boss tells you to say he's out (when he's not) it may be honest but it's not wise to say 'Mr. Smith

"God's way requires courage"

says he's out . . .' Why not say: 'I'm afraid Mr. Smith isn't available at the moment. Can I take a message?'

But there are times when you'll have to take a stand. Usually, this will mean tackling the person who is in the wrong. But try to be *loving*. Think, *'How would Jesus have coped with this?'* By following him fearlessly, you will, in fact, gain respect. Workmates don't show their respect very easily, but it's there all right.

All this is very well, but I'm unemployed . . .

Colin and *Pete* are both unemployed. They have both been in trouble in the past and have recently given their lives to Christ. Colin talks about how boring life gets and how temptation looms very large because of it. Pete seems even more fed-up. 'It's pretty rough,' he says, 'trying to run a flat when you're on the dole. You haven't got enough money. And it's frustrating when no one will take you on and you walk all over the place trying to get a job.'

I have never been unemployed and find it hard to imagine what it must be like. If you're unfortunate enough to be in this position, first make sure you go regularly to the Labour Exchange or Youth Employment, as well as scanning your local paper for jobs. Let me suggest that you do two other things also:

1 Get together with a group of Christians, tell them all about it and together ask God to provide you with a job.

2 Try to get help from your Youth Club leader or minister or some more experienced Christian person.

If you have a job, always be on the look-out for those who are unemployed and try to help them. It can be a horribly degrading position to be in.

"Ask God about a job"

You won't get me, I'm part of the Union

'And I always get my way
When I strike for higher pay.'

The Strawbs pop group summed up Trade Unions at their worst in their hit song. Many young Christians worry about whether they should join a union because of the apparent selfishness and unreasonableness.

Unions are basically good — they protect thousands of workers from unfairness and exploitation, and justice is something dear to God's own heart. The problem is that Union meetings are usually attended by only a small number of members. Never has it been more important than it is now for Christians to get involved in Trade Unions, to vote and, when possible, to speak up in favour of justice. Far from being selfish, this is a real way of showing practical concern and love for a neighbour (at work).

This is just another aspect of putting Christianity into practice at work.

Life at school, too

Even if you're not at work yet, it's pretty well certain

that you will have to be one day. Ask God to prepare you for it.

Many of the things mentioned in connection with work apply at school, too — the need for honesty and being different, for instance. And, perhaps, being conscientious shows up most of all.

While at school, you discover gradually what abilities God has given you. If you are what is called 'academic' and can cope with school work, well, it is a sign that your abilities lie in this direction. In this case, it is your responsibility to work hard and to obtain the best qualifications you can; otherwise you are neglecting the gifts which God has given you. However, if you don't seem to be very good 'academically', fair enough! Leave school as soon as you can and get a job, accepting that God has made you that way.

If you're in doubt about which category you come in, trust in God becomes very important. He will use many different ways of guiding you (including your school careers teacher).

I was talking to Steve about this. He was all set to leave school, aged sixteen, having got some 'O' levels and having got a job on the railways. At the last moment, the job fell through, and he went back to school. He emerged, two years later, with some 'A' levels — and then went on the railways! However, he is now (some seven or eight years later) entering theological college to train for the ministry — and very relieved that he has those 'A' levels already under his belt. He almost missed the boat — or, rather, the train!

Jesus said: 'I will be with you always.' (Matthew 28.20) That is in the school, the factory, the office, the sewage works, wherever you are.

FREE TIME AND ALL THAT

Jesus once gave a fabulous summary of his purposes for our lives — 'I have come in order that you might have life, life in all its fullness.' (John 10.10)

Compare this with the image most people get: 'Christianity is not for me — it's too boring and there are too many things to give up.'

Ever heard anyone say that? I come across it often. And it's usually our fault — it's the impression we give of life with Jesus Christ.

One important part of life with Jesus Christ is *our time off*, our leisure time. And there can be no doubt that this is how God intends it to be. It's the time when we *choose what to do*, when we can really be ourselves. It shouldn't be boring at all. It should be full of good things.

Perhaps this is a new idea to you: your time, and especially your free time, has been given to you by God. *Your time isn't yours: it's God's.* There are two things he wants you to do with it:

1 Enjoy it.
2 Use it sensibly.

1 Enjoy God's time

It's completely wrong to think that when you become a Christian, you lose all your fun. *God is not a spoil-sport.* If other Christians have given you the impression that he is, they're wrong. God is involved in every little part of life — not just the 'religious bit'. St. Paul knew that, all right. To his young friend, Timothy, he wrote:

'Everything that God has created is good; nothing is to be rejected, but everything is to be received with a prayer of thanks ... God generously gives us everything for our enjoyment.' (1 Timothy 4.4; 6.17)

Eileen has been a Christian for a few years now and she is up to her eyeballs in Christian work — youth club, Sunday School, choir, Church Council, etc., etc. She really enjoys all this and longs to see people brought to faith in the Lord

Jesus. But Eileen is apt to get a little browned off. If she's not careful, 'all church work and no play can make Eileen a dull girl'.

One Sunday morning, Eileen was looking perky. It turned out that the night before, a couple of friends had taken her out ten-pin bowling and she'd really enjoyed it. 'We Christians can enjoy ourselves — we aren't just concerned about the soul,' she said.

If we don't enjoy our leisure time, there's something wrong. With shorter working hours, we're likely to get more and more time off. See it as God's gift to you, and enjoy it. But you won't really be able to enjoy it unless you . . .

2 Use God's time sensibly

It helps to carve up your time into three sections. *Some for God*. A Christian needs to spend time worshipping God. This will mean meeting with other Christians and also trying to get alone with God. As we have said, it's God's time anyway, and it's only right that he should have first pick when we decide how to spend it.

Some for others. People in need are all around us and the commandment says that we should love these people as ourselves — this obviously includes our own family as a high priority. It may take you on a visit to hospital or a Union meeting, to an evening's baby-sitting or to a protest march. But it springs from the needs of other people, as a desire to care and bring about justice.

Some for yourself. It's not wrong to care for yourself — only to do so at the expense of everyone else. What are your needs? Enough sleep (it's vital, this, but we don't like to admit it!) . . . food . . . exercise . . . recreation — something which does you good. (It can be almost anything — a football match, dressmaking, servicing a car or motor-bike, going to the pictures, cooking, reading Shakespeare, etc. It depends on your own taste. Praise God, we're all different!

It looks as if only part of this is for God but, in fact, even those parts which are for others and ourselves are really for him. He is Lord of all — therefore Lord of our free time.

> "God is Lord of all"

Two important matters

Holidays are a good example of free time: it's worth giving some thought to the best way of spending the week or weeks at your disposal.

I cannot recommend too strongly going on a Christian holiday, whether a 'houseparty' or — if you're feeling energetic — a 'workparty'. Such ventures are likely to be advertised at your Church, especially if you have a Youth Fellowship. Obviously, your family must give you the go-ahead (sometimes parents are pleased to have a rest from their children — 'absence makes the heart grow fonder!'). But there are so many advantages.

Being with other Christians for a solid period of time

gives you a great chance to 'grow up' as a Christian. You can get to know God better, help other people, and have a first-rate holiday yourself — all in one go.

Money: 'What do you like doing in your free time, Kenny?'

'Spending my money!'

If work is when we can earn money, free time is when we decide what to do with it. Like using our time, this is a big responsibility.

Remember: *our money is not ours; it's God's* (just like our time). He has given it to us to look after and use in the best way we can.

Remember too: *money is good*. It's only when used in the wrong way, or when it becomes too important to you, that it is wrong — just like sex, come to think of it. '*The love* of money is the root of all evil,' the Bible says, and *not* 'money is the root of all evil.'

So, the important thing is to ask yourself: '*What good can I do with my money?*' Let me suggest some really good things:—

Give some away. 'God loves a cheerful giver,' the Bible says. There is so much need all around us. See page 26.

"Give generously, spend carefully"

Save some. If you can discipline yourself to do this regularly, one day you'll be grateful. Perhaps you'll want to get married or buy a house or something else that costs a lot of money. The thing is to open an account at a Post Office or Building Society, or else have a deposit account at a Bank. Pay a little in regularly — it mounts up!

Spend some — but take care! Most people spend generously and give away carefully. The Christian should be the opposite: he should give generously and spend very carefully.

We have seen that leisure is a very good thing, given to us by God, to be enjoyed and to be used sensibly. As with all good things, it has *danger*. Such as . . .

Danger 1: Selfishness.

Until we die, we shall have a constant battle over who is 'Number One' in our lives. Our own selfish desires (with no concern for God, no concern for the needs of others) so easily take control.

Example: You have a boyfriend or girlfriend, just to be 'successful' and well thought of, just to get what pleasure you can. In fact, you are 'using' someone for your own purposes.

Even when you're enjoying time off, you are still a Christian. You still have to answer to God for how you spend it.

Danger 2: Materialism.

This is a big evil of our day. Things, possessions, aren't wrong in themselves — but they have become gods. They become more and more important to us.

Example: What about clothes? Obviously a Christian shouldn't look dowdy but the danger is often for young people to spend huge amounts of money, time and effort in chasing after trendiness. For many it's not even a question of 'trendiness comes next to godliness' — it comes far ahead of it!

What a contrast there is between all this grabbing after material things and the life of Jesus. He lived such a simple life — and he taught his followers to do the same. 'Why worry about clothes?' he asked. 'Look how the wild flowers grow: they do not work or make clothes for themselves. But I tell you that not even King Solomon with all his wealth had clothes as beautiful as one of these flowers. It is God who clothes the wild grass . . . Won't he be all the more sure to clothe you? How little faith you have!' (Matthew 6.28–30)

Don't worry about things, says Jesus. 'Instead, give first place to his kingdom and to what he requires, and he will provide you with all these other things'. Put God first!

Danger 3: Forgetfulness.

Far from putting God first, we often forget him; we try to leave him right out of our lives.

Example: The 'party' season. One year, our Youth Fellowship arranged to have a party to celebrate Christmas. The first half was innocent enough, but during the second half the lights were very dim and the mistletoe took over. They had *forgotten* whose birthday they were celebrating. What if the Lord Jesus had appeared suddenly? The partner-swapping 'snoggers' and the 'boozers' would have been embarrassed, to put it mildly.

That's quite a test when it comes to spending our leisure time. How would I feel if suddenly I saw Jesus standing by me? Could I carry on with an easy conscience? If so, I'm enjoying it as he intends. If not, I'll have fallen into one of the dangers.

1 How much time do you waste every day? Doing what?
2 Do you think that any harm can come from listening constantly to pop music? Could it cause any of the dangers mentioned above?
3 Read Matthew 6.28–33. What do the words of Jesus say to our generation?

Things to think and talk about

FRIENDS OF JESUS

There's something great about counting an important person as your friend. At school, the hero who scores a hat-trick in an important school match is in great demand as a personal friend. Or the girl who takes the lead in a school play; the local person who makes good in some way or other.

When Joe Cocker first topped the charts as a pop singer, I lived just a few streets away from where he used to live in Sheffield. All the Youth Club were saying, 'I know Joe Cocker . . . I used to be in the scouts with him . . .' Yet now, Joe Cocker probably wouldn't know any of them.

But it *is* possible to get a genuine thrill out of being counted a friend of Jesus Christ. 'You are my friends,' he said to his disciples.

Just think for a moment who Jesus is: *Son of God, King of Kings* and *Lord of Lords*. And yet, he is interested in individual people; he wants to enjoy a relationship with us. He wants to be our friend, an utterly dependable friend who won't forget us, even though he is the greatest of all celebrities. As it says at the very beginning of this book, when Jesus is our friend we *belong* to him and he *belongs* to us.

So, the message is:

Make the most of this friendship!

Look at a tree. Even in the middle of a big city, you shouldn't have to go far to see one. Then focus on one twig. Then imagine *you* are that twig. As long as you stay part of the tree, there's life in you. But your life depends on staying part of the tree.

Jesus was talking about this to his followers in front of a 'grape tree' (usually called a vine!). 'I am the vine, and you are the branches. Whoever remains in me, and I in him, will bear much fruit; for you can do nothing without me,' he told them. (John 15.5) So, just as the twig has to stay part of the tree to survive, and be of any use at all, so the Christian has to stay part of Jesus for the same reason.

Stay *joined* to Jesus. The older versions of the Bible say 'abide' in him. Sadly, the word 'abide' has gone out of currency without being replaced. We'll settle for the phrase 'stuck on' to Jesus. If we want to take advantage of being a friend of Jesus, we have to keep in touch with him, *stuck on* to him, the whole time. Wherever we go, whatever we're doing, Jesus is with us, and, if we are real friends, we welcome his presence.

How does this work out?

It may sound fine in theory, but can it be done? It depends on learning one precious secret — praying with your eyes open! A Christian has a built-in walkie-talkie which gets him straight through to God at all times. And he likes us to talk to him at any time about anything.

Why not try it now? Go out in the street and turn whoever or whatever you see into a prayer.

... *masses of litter on the pavement*. 'Lord, help us to look after the world you have given us. May people stop dropping all this litter.'

... *it's raining*. 'Lord, I don't like rain at all, but please help me to be cheerful, whatever it's like.'

... *a car with a huge dent in its side*. 'Lord, help all drivers to drive carefully. Protect us from accidents, especially our Paul as he drives home tonight.'

... *an old lady carrying a heavy basket of shopping*. 'Lord, help old people, and help us Christians who are still young to help them.'

... *three lads and a girl, all wearing Manchester City scarves*. 'Lord, thank you for football. Thank you for all the pleasure I get from it — and thousands of others, too. Thank you that we've got the best team in the country . . . .'

You see, there's no end to the possibilities. It is a habit to develop. There's nothing that your friend, the Lord Jesus, isn't interested in — nothing at all.

Just one thing spoils this amazing relationship. When

we displease him by something we think, say or do, then the reception on the walkie-talkie gets more and more crackled. We usually call this *sin* and the result of sin. A lot of Christians get really bothered about this. *'Am I still a Christian if I sin?'* The answer, thankfully, is 'Yes'. (Just as well — there hasn't been a Christian who hasn't sinned!) *But your friendship with God is temporarily spoilt.*

If you hurt any other friend, the only way to make it up is to say sorry. The same applies with Jesus. And the quicker we do so, the better. Don't let 'unconfessed' sins mount up; admit them to him, say sorry and accept his amazing forgiveness. Immediately, the friendship is restored and the crackles on the line disappear. (For more about this problem of sin, every Christian's hang-up, see the section on *Failure.*)

"Keep talking to God"

When a Christian is using his walkie-talkie as a continuous habit, it is a fantastic help when temptation to sin comes along. Go out into the street again. Who do you see?

. . . the man who swore at you when you accidentally bumped into him yesterday. You feel hatred as soon as you see him. But — 'Lord, help me to love that bloke. Help me not to hate him. Lord, you love him. You love all of us even though we've all hurt you.'

. . . a really beautiful girl (assume for this once, that you're a fella!) What do you do now? 'Lord, you made her — thank you for making her so gorgeous. Help me keep my thoughts clean.'

Big deal, you may think! But it works. It really does.

A story.

Jesus' followers were crossing the Sea of Galilee in a boat when a great storm blew up. In the middle of the night, they thought they saw a ghost walking on the water, until he spoke — 'It is I. Don't be afraid.' Was it really Jesus? Simon Peter put it to the test and strode across the water to him. He suddenly noticed the wind, the waves, the danger. He looked down and began to sink. 'Save me, Lord!' he cried. At once, Jesus reached out and grabbed him.

Look at the temptation and you'll sink!
Reach out to Jesus and he'll grab you!
You can read the story in Matthew, chapter 14.22–33.

Summary

Think of the tree. **Keep stuck on.**
Think of the walkie-talkie. **Keep in touch.**
Think of walking on the water. **Keep reaching out.**

Things to discuss or think about

1 John, chapter 15 (or some of it).
2 At what time is it really hard to keep *stuck on* to Jesus?
3 What can help you to remember that Jesus is with you all the time? A knot in your handkerchief?
4 How would you describe a real friend? Does Jesus qualify?